SPORTS SCIENCE

Tennis

Patricia Bow

W

FRANKLIN WATTS

LONDON • SYDNEY

This edition first published in 2013
by Franklin Watts

Copyright © 2013
Brown Bear Books Ltd

Franklin Watts
338 Euston Road
London NW1 3BH

Franklin Watts Australia
Level 17/207 Kent Street
Sydney, NSW 2000

A CIP catalogue record for this book is available
from the British Library.

Dewey no: 796.342

ISBN 978 1 4451 2356 1

Printed in China

Franklin Watts is a division of Hachette Children's Books,
an Hachette UK company.
www.hachette.co.uk

Note to parents and teachers concerning websites:
In the book every effort has been made by the Publishers to
ensure that websites are suitable for children, that they are
of the highest educational value, and that they contain no
inappropriate or offensive material. However, because of the
nature of the Internet, it is impossible to guarantee that the
contents of these sites will not be altered. We advise that
Internet access is supervised by a responsible adult.

For Brown Bear Books Ltd:
Designer: Lynne Lennon
Picture Researcher: Sean Hannaway
Editor: Leon Gray
Managing Editor: Tim Cooke
Art Director: Jeni Child
Design Manager: David Poole
Children's Publisher: Anne O'Daly
Editorial Director: Lindsey Lowe

Every effort has been made to trace the owners
of copyrighted material.

Photo credits

Front cover: Phil Anthony/Shutterstock
Backgrounds: Galina Barskaya/Shutterstock

Action Images: Jason O'Brien 4–5, 20, Antoine Couvercelle 7t,
Virginie Bouyer 7b, Kevin Lamarque 12–13, Michael Regan 13t,
Tim Wimbourne 14–15, Kimberly White 19, Livepic 23t, Alessia
Pierdomenico 26; Action Plus: Neil Tingle 15t, Steve Bardens 17t;
Alamy: Art of Advertising 9b; Corbis: Reuters 11t; Getty Images:
Julian Finney 8, Hulton 9t, Jacques Demarthon 23b, Kaneja
Muganda 24, Patrick Lin 25t, Ryan Pierse 25b; Mary Evans
Picture Library: 5t; PA Photos: John Giles 10, Sean Dempsey 11b,
Lynne Sladky 15b, Zuma Press 22–23, Alastair Grant 29b;
Photolibrary Group: Aflo Foto Agency 5r; Rex Features: Nils
Jorgensen 28; Shutterstock: Jose Gil 16l, 16r, 17bl, 17br, Olga
Besnard 21t, 27b, James M. Phelps Jr 21b, Vasily Smirnov 27t,
Olga Bogatyrenko 29t; Wilson: 13cl, 13c, 13cr.

Illustrations: Mark Walker 6, 18

Contents

Introducing Tennis

Tennis was once a game for kings. Today, nearly fifty million people in almost every country around the world play this popular sport.

People played an early version of tennis around 700 years ago. Modern tennis began in 1873 in England. At first, tennis was an amateur sport. In the 1960s, the major tournaments opened up to professionals. Today, Rafael Nadal, Maria Sharapova and other top players are as famous as pop stars.

Rules of the game

Modern tennis is a lightning-fast, hard-hitting game. The sport is played on surfaces ranging from grass to **acrylic**. The players are strong, well-trained athletes. They use stringed rackets to hit a ball over a net. Two players make up a singles game. Two teams of two players make up a doubles game. A player starts by serving. He or she stands behind the **baseline** at the back of the court and hits the ball over the net. His or her opponent tries to hit the ball back.

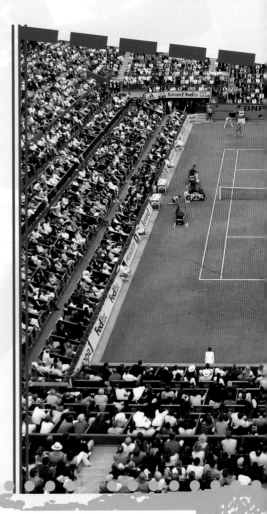

Spectators watch a game at the Roland-Garros stadium in Paris, France.

NEW WORDS

Acrylic: A type of plastic with many different uses.

LOOK CLOSER

Real tennis

'Real' tennis began in France 700 years ago. King Henry VIII of England was a keen player. About 6,000 people still play this older game, which uses a hard ball and wooden rackets in walled courts (see left).

▶ ▶ ▶ ▶ ▶ ▶ ▶ ▶

FACT!

What's in a name?

In tennis, zero points is called 'love'. This word may come from the French word *l'oeuf,* which means 'egg'. This refers to the shape of the numeral '0'.

➡ *Many people play tennis to keep fit and meet friends.*

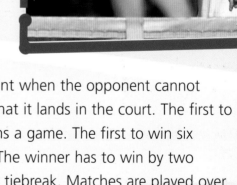

Scoring

A player wins a point when the opponent cannot return the ball so that it lands in the court. The first to win four points wins a game. The first to win six games wins a set. The winner has to win by two games or there is a tiebreak. Matches are played over the best of three or five sets.

Baseline: The line marking the back of the court.

Holding Court

Tennis courts are usually made of clay, grass or hard surfaces such as acrylic. Grass is rarest – the upkeep takes work and money. Centre Court at Wimbledon in London is the most famous grass court in the world.

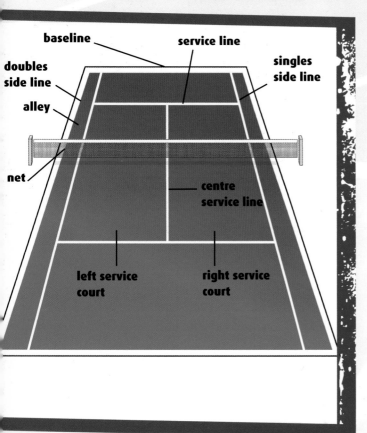

- baseline
- service line
- doubles side line
- singles side line
- alley
- net
- centre service line
- left service court
- right service court

Clay courts are made of crushed, hard-packed stone (green clay) or brick (red clay). The courts at Stade Roland-Garros in Paris, France, are crushed brick on a base of crushed pebbles, ash and limestone. Hard courts are no longer plain asphalt or concrete. For example, the Australian Open at Melbourne is played on courts made of layers of rubber-filled acrylic.

Fast and slow

Clay courts are 'slow', because the gritty surface creates a lot of **friction**

◄ *The court is clearly marked with a series of white lines.*

NEW WORDS

Friction: The drag created when two surfaces slide across each other.

The courts at Flushing Meadows in New York are made of layers of hard rubber over asphalt.

LOOK CLOSER

Court care

Wimbledon uses tough rye grass. The courts are rolled and covered each day to keep the soil firm and dry, and mown to keep the grass 8 mm (⅓ inch) tall.

with the ball. Friction slows down the ball and makes it bounce higher. This gives the **receiver** more time to reach the ball and play the returning shot. Grass courts are 'fast'. The ball skids over the surface of the grass, bouncing low and fast. It is easier to win a quick point on grass because the receiver has less time to react. Hard courts are faster than clay, but slower than grass.

Measuring up

A tennis court is 24.4 by 8.5 metres (78 x 27 ft). For doubles, extra space on the sides makes the court 11.25 metres (36 ft) wide. The net is 1 metre (3 ft) high at the centre. Sidelines, baseline and other areas are marked in white. These show where the ball goes 'out'.

The roof opens to make this indoor court an outdoor court.

▶▶▶▶▶▶▶▶
Grand Slam

FACT!

The 'Grand Slam' comprises four tournaments: Wimbledon and the Australian, French, and U.S. Opens. Martina Navratilova has won the most Grand Slams — a world record 18 victories.

Receiver: The player who is trying to return the ball.

Making a Racket

For hundreds of years, tennis rackets were made of wood. In 1967, the rackets were made lighter and stronger when steel and aluminium designs came on to the market. Modern **graphite** rackets are even better. Players can swing them faster and hit the ball harder.

Graphite frames can be made larger than wooden ones. This creates a larger 'sweet spot'. The larger the sweet spot, the easier it is to hit the ball hard and well. Swedish tennis legend Bjorn Borg used a wooden racket to win 11 Grand Slam titles in the 1970s and 1980s. In 1991 he made a comeback using a wooden racket. A low-ranked player with a graphite racket beat him easily.

Graphite rackets have made tennis a fast, action-packed sport.

NEW WORDS

Graphite: Carbon fibre mixed with resin and other materials such as Kevlar and titanium.

FACT!

▶ ▶ ▶ ▶ ▶ ▶ ▶ ▶ ▶

Gut feeling

The strings of tennis rackets used to be made from of the lining of (usually) cow intestines. 'Gut' is still highly prized for its bounce and the way it softens vibrations. However, modern artificial strings are replacing gut string. Players often combine types of strings on the same racket. Roger Federer uses polyester Luxilon and natural gut.

Racket size

Tennis rackets are between 67.5 and 72.5 centimetres (27–29 in) long. The International Tennis Federation (ITF) has strict rules for the rackets used in professional matches. The racket cannot have more than 675 square centimetres (135 in^2) of head area. However, professional players usually play with heavier, smaller rackets. This helps them hit the ball with precision and control exactly where the ball goes.

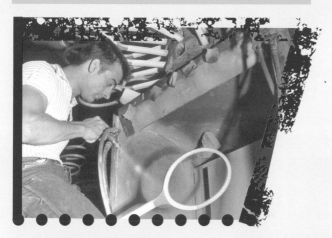

◀ *Early tennis rackets were always made from wood.*

▼ *Machines string tennis rackets to impart the perfect tension.*

LOOK CLOSER

Highly strung

Tennis professionals may have their rackets restrung after each match. String **tension** is very important. Tighter strings bite into the ball for a more controlled shot. Looser strings give a stronger shot. When the ball hits the loose strings, they give way and then spring back, which adds energy to the ball.

Tension: How tight or loose the strings are on a tennis racket.

New Balls Please

A woman inspects a batch of tennis balls to ensure high quality standards.

A tennis ball is made with a hollow rubber core, which is filled with gas under pressure. Fuzzy **Melton** cloth is then glued on the outside.

A tennis ball is bouncy because the gas inside it pushes against the inner walls of the ball. When the ball hits a racket, the pressure makes it bounce.

Ball change

Tennis balls lose their bounce quickly. At professional tournaments, ball changes occur after the warm up,

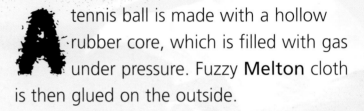

LOOK CLOSER

Ball standard

At professional tournaments, the balls are tested regularly for bounce, weight, and size. The balls must bounce between 132.5 and 145 centimetres (53–58 inches) after being dropped onto concrete from a height of 2.5 metres (8⅓ feet).

NEW WORDS

Melton: Tough fabric with a fuzzy texture. Melton consists of wool with a little viscose or nylon.

▶▶▶▶▶▶▶▶

Line up

About 360 million tennis balls are manufactured each year. This many balls would form a line 23,265 kilometres (14,540 miles) long, stretching from London to New York City four times.

⬆ *Balls are stored in sealed cans so they do not lose their bounce.*

the first seven games and then after every nine games. It helps to keep balls at a steady temperature. Warm balls bounce higher than cold ones because the pressure of a gas in an enclosed space goes up as the temperature rises. At Wimbledon, the match balls are kept in a special container at 20°C (68°F).

Fuzzy balls

The balls are covered with the fuzzy Melton cloth for a purpose. The fuzz catches the air and increases **drag**. This makes the ball spin. Without spin, you would not see the curved shots that play such a big part in tennis. Being hit so many times is hard on the fuzz,

⬆ *Regular ball changes ensure that the players use the bounciest balls.*

which gets fluffy. Fluffy balls bounce oddly, so players check them before they serve and toss away the fluffiest.

Drag: The pull of the air on an object.

Tennis Gear

Tennis players move with sudden sprints, turns and jumps. A player sprints and then plants his or her foot down to stop. This creates a force up to four times the weight of the player's body.

Tennis shoes are designed to keep players from being injured by these explosive movements. Support at the heel, sides and ankle keeps the foot from slipping, rolling or twisting. **Polyurethane** foam in the sole absorbs the shock. Mesh insets in the leather keep the feet cool and dry and prevent blisters.

Different shoes are made for playing on different surfaces. Grass-court shoes have rubber studs on the soles to give a good grip without tearing up the soil. Clay court shoes have a zigzag tread pattern for good **traction** on the gritty surface. The same pattern, only deeper for harder wear, is found on hard court shoes.

What to wear?

Tennis clothing is made from new materials that let the body move freely. They help keep the player cool,

At Wimbledon, players must wear white clothing.

NEW WORDS

Polyurethane: A synthetic rubberlike substance.

▲ **Tennis shoes absorb the shock of the player's movements.**

FACT!

▶ ▶ ▶ ▶ ▶ ▶ ▶ ▶

Sleeveless success

The 2008 Wimbledon men's singles champion Rafael Nadal always wears sleeveless tops with knee-length shorts.

clay

hard court

grass

Tennis shoes have different soles for different surfaces.

LOOK CLOSER

Fantastic fabrics

Modern tennis clothes are made of new fabrics such as Nike's Dri-FIT. This blend of cotton and polyester absorbs sweat from the skin and keeps it away from the body. Some fabrics are treated with titanium dioxide. This mineral scatters ultraviolet radiation from the sun.

keep sweat away from the body and protect from the sun's harmful rays.

Fashion statement

At the 2002 U.S. Open, Serena Williams wore a black, leather-look body suit she had designed herself. In 2004, she caused a stir with a jewelled tank top and denim miniskirt.

Traction: The grip of the shoe on the ground.

Cutting-Edge Technology

Powerful rackets and strong, athletic players have made tennis a fast-paced sport. Umpires and line judges cannot always tell if a ball is in or out. But a single point can win or lose a match.

A service line judge signals to the umpire that the ball is out of play.

In 1980, Cyclops was brought in to help the judges make the right calls. Cyclops is a machine that uses electronic beams to detect where the ball lands. It beeps loudly to signal that the ball is out of play.

Hawk-Eye

In 2006, a system called Hawk-Eye arrived. It is now used at most major tournaments. It was used at the 2008 Beijing Olympics. Hawk-Eye uses ten video cameras to track every shot. A computer processes the

FACT!

▶ ▶ ▶ ▶ ▶ ▶ ▶ ▶ ▶

Speedy Service

Radar guns measured the average service speed by the top men at Wimbledon in 2007 at 191.5 km/h (119 mph). Women at the U.S. Open in 2007 had an average service speed of 157 km/h (97.6 mph).

NEW WORDS

Radar: A way of detecting objects by sending out a signal and measuring the signal that bounces back.

LOOK CLOSER

Speed of the serve

At major tournaments like Wimbledon, **radar** sensors at each end of the court measure the speed of serves. The sensor emits a silent signal that hits the oncoming ball and bounces back. The returning signal is changed in a way that depends on how fast the ball is moving. This change is called the Doppler shift. A computer uses the information to figure out the speed of the serve.

images and creates **3-D** pictures to show how the ball landed. A screen displays the images around the court. Most players and spectators like the new system. Umpires and line judges still make the calls, but Hawk-Eye acts as a back-up system to catch bad calls. Other players, such as the Swiss tennis champion Roger Federer, are not so happy. They point out that Hawk-Eye, too, can make mistakes.

A net-cord sensor detects serves that touch the net.

➡️ *Hawk-Eye tracks the movement of the ball to create 3-D images on a computer screen.*

3-D: Three dimensions — having depth as well as width and height.

Service

The player who serves first has an advantage. It is very hard to return a skilled, powerful serve.

During service, a player stands with one foot behind the service line, facing towards his or her opponent. The server then tosses the ball up above his or her head and whips the racket from behind and up at the ball in a long, smooth motion. At the same time, the server moves forwards onto the front foot. He or she stretches to hit the ball as high and hard as possible. The racket then moves down and across the front of the body.

During service, the player aims to hit the ball as quickly and as accurately as possible.

NEW WORDS

Ace: Serve where the receiver fails to return or even touch the ball.

▶ ▶ ▶ ▶ ▶ ▶ ▶ ▶

FACT!

Fastest serve

Andy Roddick set the world record for the fastest serve – 247 km/h (153.5 mph) – in June 2004 at the Queen's Club in London. Venus Williams set the fastest women's serve at the 2007 U.S. Open – 207.6 km/h (129 mph).

Take your chance

The server gets two serves. Most players hope to win the point from a powerful first serve. If the first serve fails, the second is hit with more care. The aim is to ensure the ball lands in the right service box – the one on the opposite side of the court from the server.

Fault

If the ball hits the net or lands outside the service box, the umpire calls a fault. Two faults results in a double fault, and the receiver wins the point. If the ball lands inside the service box and the receiver does not reach it, that's called an **ace**. The server wins a point.

LOOK CLOSER

Energy transfer

When a ball hits a hard surface it flattens and then bounces. At the same time, it lets off energy in the form of heat and sound. The more energy lost, the less the ball will bounce. But racket strings are even more **elastic** than the ball. The strings stretch so the ball does not flatten as much or lose as much energy. The strings then snap back, adding energy to the ball.

Elastic: The ability of materials to regain their original shape after being deformed by stress.

Key Strokes

Most shots are played after the ball has bounced once. You can play all 'ground strokes' either **forehand** or **backhand**. Spin can turn a normal stroke into a surprise attack.

Topspin lets a tennis player hit the ball really hard, but with less risk that it will go out of play. To create topspin, the racket starts low and moves up as it hits the ball, with the top edge slanted forwards. The ball drops fast, just past the net, and then bounces high.

Slicing shots

Backspin, or slice, is the opposite of topspin. The racket starts high and moves down as it hits the ball, with the bottom edge slanted

➡ Players use different grips to play different shots.

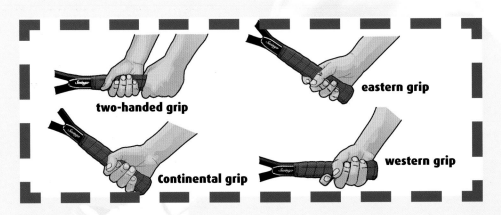

two-handed grip

eastern grip

Continental grip

western grip

NEW WORDS

Forehand: Holding the racket out to the side with the front of the arm forwards.

18

LOOK CLOSER

Topspin

When the racket hits the ball, it gives it a small upward push. As the ball flies across the court, the top of the ball spins forwards against the flow of air. The air on top bunches up and flows more slowly. Air pressure builds up on top of the ball. Pressure forces the ball downwards. This is called the Magnus effect.

French tennis player Marion Bartoli hits a double-handed backhand shot.

forwards. The ball sails high into the back of the court. When it lands, the ball bounces at a low angle, forcing the receiver to dive to make the return.

▶ ▶ ▶ ▶ ▶ ▶ ▶ ▶

FACT!

Left handers

Left-handed players may have an edge over right-handers, making them play strokes from unexpected directions. Jimmy Connors, John McEnroe, Martina Navratilova and Monica Seles are left-handed players. Spanish champion Rafael Nadal plays with his left hand but is really right-handed!

Grip matters

Different ways of holding the racket are better for different shots. The eastern grip is good for most shots. The semi-western grip tilts the face of the racket down slightly. This helps create topspin. When you hold the racket like an axe, it is called a chopper grip. It lets you swing the racket more powerfully and is often used during service.

Backhand: Holding the racket across your body with the back of the arm forwards.

Shot Variations

A player stretches to play a half volley.

Different tennis shots are best suited to different situations.

A lob is played with enough backspin to sail high into the back of the court. The best time to play a lob shot is when your opponent is near the net. He or she will have to jump high or run back to return the ball.

Drop shot

The drop shot is a softer shot played with topspin. Done right, it drops the ball just over the net. A good time to play it is when your opponent is near the baseline.

The volley

To volley, you hit the ball before it has had time to bounce. You must be near the net to play a volley. This is risky. You could surprise your opponent

NEW WORDS

Overhead smash: A powerful forehand shot made the same way as a serve.

FACT!

Slow down

A ball served by Andy Roddick leaves his racket at 193 km/h (120 mph). It slows to about 96.5 km/h (60 mph) just before it lands.

← Volleys are played near the net.

and win a point. But if your opponent reaches the ball, he or she may lob it to the baseline.

Half volley

The half volley is played just after the ball has bounced. There is a risk this ball could pop up high. If it does, your opponent might hit an **overhead smash**. To avoid **pop-ups**, make the shot with the racket face tilted slightly downward.

LOOK CLOSER

Forces at work

As a lobbed ball sails high above the court, several forces are at work. Lift is the upwards pressure created by backspin and pushes the ball up. Thrust is the forwards momentum that carries the ball forwards. Drag is the force of the air against the ball, slowing it down. The force of gravity pulls the ball down to the ground on a gentle curve.

↑ A drop shot is a soft stroke that dips over the net.

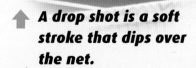

Pop-up: A short, high shot without much power.

Nutrition

ood **nutrition** and hydration keep tennis players fit for the game.

Players eat complex carbohydrates for energy. These carbohydrates are in wholegrain breads, cereals, fruit, pasta and potatoes. The body uses them to make glucose – a type of sugar that supplies the body with energy. Glucose also keeps the blood sugar levels in check, preventing people from getting tired too quickly. Tennis players eat protein to build muscle. The best protein foods are low-fat yogurt and milk, meat, fish, beans and tofu.

Eating healthy

Professional players eat a healthy diet all year. A few days before a match, they eat more carbohydrates to raise the body's glycogen levels. The day before a match they will eat a high-carbohydrate, high-protein, low-fat main meal. An hour or so before a match they will eat a high-carbohydrate snack such as yogurt or a cereal bar. Players fuel up on carbohydrates after a match to keep blood sugar from falling too low.

Breakfast is the most important meal of the day.

NEW WORDS

Nutrition: How good food builds a strong and healthy body and brain.

22

LOOK CLOSER

Go bananas!

Rafael Nadal and Maria Sharapova (pictured) eat bananas on the court. Bananas contain a lot of vitamins and minerals. They have complex sugars for energy. One of those sugars makes bananas very digestible.

▶ ▶ ▶ ▶ ▶ ▶ ▶

FACT!

Calorie count

A tennis player can easily burn 1,000 to 1,440 calories during a two-hour match.

Fluid intake

Athletes need plenty of water to replace the water lost through sweat. Sweat keeps the body cool. During a tennis match, a player can lose 3 litres (5 pints) of sweat each hour. If this water is not replaced, the player will become dehydrated. He or she feels tired, and the muscles cramp. Extreme dehydration is dangerous. Trained players drink more a day or two before a match and well after the match. Sports drinks are a good choice. They have water, carbohydrates for energy and **electrolytes** to prevent cramps.

➡ ***Powdered sports drinks are mixed with water.***

Electrolyte: Salt is an example of an electrolyte. It breaks up into charged ions when it dissolves in water.

Fighting Fit

Tennis players are all-round athletes. They have the strength to make powerful serves and returns. They can sprint at top speed from a standing start and leap and lunge to reach the ball. And they have the **stamina** to keep playing for hours.

Tennis has come a long way in the past 30 years. Players are making harder shots, but they are getting more injuries.The most common tennis injuries are in the shoulders, back and joints. A small injury can cost a player a match. A bad injury could end his or her career. Players work with physical trainers to stay at the top of their game.

Young players learn their skills in a tennis academy.

NEW WORDS

Stamina: The ability to keep working or playing for a long time without getting tired.

▶ ▶ ▶ ▶ ▶ ▶ ▶ ▶

FACT! Heart Rate

At rest, the hearts of most people beat between 60 and 80 times a minute. A tennis player's resting heart rate is lower, because the heart is stronger. Bjorn Borg's resting heart rate is 35 beats per minute — one of the lowest of all the tennis players past and present.

The trainer helps the player plan a set of exercises to improve skills, build fitness and prevent injury.

Strength and stamina

Players train with weights to build strength. They might do short sprints to improve **agility**. They use plyometrics to sprint quickly. Plyometrics are exercises such as squat jumps, which train the muscles to move with explosive power. Stamina relies on a strong heart to carry oxygen to hard-working muscles. Players do aerobic (oxygen-burning) exercise such as long-distance running or cycling to build stamina.

Hopping between a series of lines improves agility.

Push ups build strong muscles in the upper body.

LOOK CLOSER

Aerobic and anaerobic

During a long match, the muscles use up a lot of oxygen to get energy from glucose. This is aerobic activity. When sprinting, muscles work so hard that they take in glucose without increasing oxygen consumption. This is anaerobic activity.

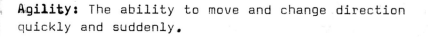

Agility: The ability to move and change direction quickly and suddenly.

All in the Mind

Playing professional tennis can be very stressful. There is a lot at stake. A player's place in the world **rankings** depends on winning.

The stress is partly physical. A long match might last for up to four hours. The longest Wimbledon match was the 2008 men's singles final. Rafael Nadal defeated Roger Federer after 4 hours and 48 minutes. Noise from the crowd, strong wind and sunlight and unbearable heat add more stress. Worst of all is a bad **line call**. It is easy to lose concentration and get upset if you think you have lost a point unfairly. A player who gets angry or upset will not think clearly, and the muscles tense up. The player might start making mistakes, which could lose the match.

➡️ *Rafael Nadal lifts the 2008 Wimbledon trophy after playing in the longest men's singles final.*

NEW WORDS

Rankings: Official list of the best tennis players. Number 1 holds most points won in tournaments.

LOOK CLOSER

Serving rituals

Before serving, Maria Sharapova always carefully tucks her hair behind her ears (left). Novak Djokovic bounces the ball up to 25 times. These rituals help players focus on their serves.

Many players have rituals – habits they repeat during the game. They may bounce the ball a few times or close their eyes. These habits calm their nerves so they can play their best.

Mental strength helps players win important matches.

Sports psychology

Some players hire sports psychologists. They help players think about playing important shots. When the time comes, the player makes the right moves without thinking. Psychologists also teach players how to stay calm. One way is to build pictures in the mind – to 'see' themselves hitting the ball.

▶ ▶ ▶ ▶ ▶ ▶ ▶

FACT!

Super Brat

U.S. former champion John McEnroe was famous for his tantrums when he thought the umpire had made a mistake. The newspapers named him 'Super Brat'.

Line call: A line judge's decision on whether a ball is in or out.

The Future of Tennis

Tennis is changing in many different ways. In the past, most top players were British, American and Australian. Now they come from all over the world.

In 2007, the Association of Tennis Professionals (ATP) top three rankings for men were Roger Federer (Swiss), Rafael Nadal (Spanish), and Novak Djokovic (Serbian). Ana Ivanovic, the top woman, also comes from Serbia.

The size of the tennis player is also changing. Today's champions are taller and stronger than the champions from 30 years ago. People used to think big tennis players were slow and clumsy. But the training is making them much fitter. Big players have better skills, and they often have stronger serves.

You can now play tennis as a virtual reality simulation.

NEW WORDS

Piezoelectric racket: A tennis racket that generates electricity when a ball hits it.

▶ ▶ ▶ ▶ ▶ ▶ ▶ ▶

FACT! Tall for tennis

Tennis players are taller than ever. Ivo Karlovic is 205 centimetres (6 ft 10 in.) John Isner (right) is 202.5 centimetres (6 ft 9 in.), and Chris Guccione is 197.5 centimetres (6 ft 7 in.) Among the women, Lindsay Davenport is 186.25 centimetres (6 ft 2½ in.), Maria Sharapova is 185 centimetres (6 ft 2 in.), and Venus Williams is 182.5 centimetres (6 ft 1 in.).

🔻 *The TEL system checks line calls using electronic wire sensors that are buried beneath the court.*

Tennis of the future

Tennis gear keeps on improving, thanks to science. The **piezoelectric racket** is a good example. When a ball hits the strings, special materials in the frame turn the vibrations into electrical energy. This softens the vibrations. Balls are turning high-tech, too. One type has a coating of clay **nanoparticles** on the inside wall. The clay keeps the pressurised air inside the ball from escaping.

High-tech tennis

Where will technology take us? Most spectators are pleased with Hawk-Eye. But we will probably still need human officials in the future – because machines, too, can make mistakes.

LOOK CLOSER

Calling the shots

The U.S. Open has installed the Tennis Electronic Line (TEL) system. This system uses special balls with a metal powder inside and wire sensors buried under the surface of the court. The sensors detect where the ball lands. A computer shows if the shot is in or out.

Nanoparticles: Particles that are just a few atoms wide – far too small to be seen with the naked eye.

Glossary

3-D: Three dimensions — having depth as well as width and height.

Ace: Serve where the receiver fails to return or even touch the ball.

Acrylic: A type of plastic with many uses.

Agility: The ability to move and change direction quickly and suddenly.

Backhand: Holding the racket across your body with the back of the arm facing forwards.

Baseline: The line at the back of the court.

Drag: The pull of the air on an object.

Friction: The drag created when two surfaces slide across each other.

Elastic: The ability of materials to regain their original shape after being deformed by stress.

Electrolyte: Salt is an example of an electrolyte. It breaks up into charged ions when it dissolves in water.

Forehand: Holding the racket out to the side with the front of the arm facing forwards.

Graphite: Carbon fibre mixed with resin and other materials such as Kevlar and titanium.

Line call: A line judge's decision on whether a ball is in or out.

Melton: Tough fabric with a fuzzy texture. Melton consists of wool and viscose or nylon.

Nanoparticles: Particles that are just a few atoms wide.

Nutrition: How good food builds a strong and healthy body and brain.

Overhead smash: A powerful forehand shot made the same way as a serve.

Piezoelectric racket: A tennis racket that generates electricity when a ball hits it.

Polyurethane: A synthetic, rubbery substance.

Pop-up: A short, high shot that lacks power.

Radar: A way of detecting objects by sending out a signal and measuring the signal that bounces back.

Rankings: Official list of the best tennis players. Number 1 holds most points won in tournaments.

Receiver: The player returning the ball.

Stamina: The ability to keep working or playing for a long time without getting tired.

Tension: How tight or loose the strings are on a tennis racket.

Traction: The grip of the shoe on the ground.

Find Out More

Books

Gifford, Clive. *Tennis (Know Your Sport)*. Franklin Watts, 2007.

Gifford, Clive. *Tennis (Inside Sport)*. Wayland, 2008.

Goodman, Polly. *Exercise and Your Body*. Wayland, 2007.

Hunter, Rebecca. *Tennis (Starting Sport)*. Franklin Watts, 2008.

Way, Edward. *Tennis (Training to Succeed)*. Franklin Watts, 2009.

Websites

The About.com website explains everything you need to know about tennis. The site includes free video lessons, practical tips and fun quizzes to test your knowledge.

http://tennis.about.com/od/instruction/Instruction_Learn_and_Improve_ Tennis_Strokes_and_Strategies.htm

This excellent online resource explores the science behind the sport of tennis.

http://wings.avkids.com/Tennis/Book/index.html

This website includes some useful articles to help improve your game.

http://www.juniortennis.com/

This BBC website teaches some tennis basics and has video masterclasses of some of the tennis greats.

http://news.bbc.co.uk/sport1/hi/tennis/skills/default.stm

Index